ROMEO AND JULIET

CONTENTS

OXFORD
UNIVERSITY PRESS

Great Clarendon Street, Oxford OX2 6DP

Oxford University Press is a department of the University of Oxford. It furthers the University's objective of excellence in research, scholarship, and education by publishing worldwide in

Oxford New York

Auckland Cape Town Dar es Salaam Hong Kong Karachi Kuala Lumpur Madrid Melbourne Mexico City Nairobi New Delhi Shanghai Taipei Toronto

With offices in

Argentina Austria Brazil Chile Czech Republic France Greece Gautamala Hungary Italy Japan South Korea Poland Portugal Singapore Switzerland Thailand Turkey Ukraine Vietnam

Oxford is a registered trade mark of Oxford University Press in the UK and in certain other countries

Text © Jenny Roberts 2008

The moral rights of the author have been asserted

Database right Oxford University Press (maker)

First published 2008

British Library Cataloguing in Publication Data

Data available

ISBN 978 019 832925 1

10 9 8 7 6 5 4 3 2 1

Printed in Great Britain by Bell and Bain Ltd., Glasgow

Acknowledgements

The publisher would like to thank the following for permission to reproduce photographs: p10 ©BHE Films; p14(top left) Bob Workman / ©RSC; p14(top right) © Joe Cocks Studio Collection Copyright Shakespeare Birthplace Trust; p14(bottom left) © Malcolm Davies Collection Copyright Shakespeare Birthplace Trust; p14(bottom right) ©Bazmark / Miramax, p15(top) ©Bazmark / Miramax; p15(middle) ©BHE Films; p15(bottom) ©Mirisch Corp

Illustrations are by Steve Evans Design and Illustration

Cover illustration by Silke Bachmann

WHAT'S IT ALL ABOUT?

Young rebels

Bloodshed and violence

Street fighting

Parties and gatecrashers

The story of Romeo and Juliet is one of the most popular stories of all time. It has been told for centuries, all over the world, and is still being retold today.

Each storyteller changes the details to suit a new audience, but the basic story is the same: two young lovers, from rival families, defy their parents and choose to die rather than be forced apart.

Daredevils

So what makes it such a great story? Well, it shows the power of young love and how it can bring together even the bitterest of enemies. When William Shakespeare told his version of the story, he gave us not only a powerful love story, but also an action-packed thriller, with a fast-paced, twisting plot, full of violence, drama, bloodshed and passion.

Fun and humour

Plots and conspiracies

Spooky settings

All the ingredients that made this play so popular in Shakespeare's time also make it popular today. Look around at some of the key features of the play. There's something to appeal to everyone, whatever their taste in entertainment!

Lies and disguises

Romance and passion

Friends and enemies

Poison and death

Wealth and power

Love and hate

The story of Romeo and Juliet is so powerful and gripping that it has been made into blockbuster films, musicals, operas and ballets. Shakespeare's play inspired many of these, and will no doubt continue to inspire young artists, writers, dancers, designers, musicians, animators, game designers and storytellers of the future. And that could be you…

FEUDING FAMILIES

What's a feud?

A **feud** is a long, bitter quarrel. It can be in any community, for example, between families, neighbours, gangs, sports supporters, tribes or clans.

FAMOUS FEUDS

Here are some famous feuds. Choose one and find out more about it.

- **Al Capone and 'Bugs' Moran**: American gangsters in Chicago, leading to the St Valentine's Day Massacre in 1929.
- **The Yorks and Lancastrians**: two rich, powerful families who fought to rule England during the War of the Roses 1455–1487.
- **The Campbells and MacDonalds**: two Scottish clans involved in the Glen Coe Massacre, 1692.

Add some more feuds to the list (they can be fictional or real feuds).

SETTING THE SCENE

Shakespeare's play starts with an introduction by 'Chorus'. Traditionally this was a group of people, but was sometimes just one actor. His job was to get the audience's attention (often tricky in an Elizabethan theatre where people would be chatting, eating and milling around the stage). With no scenery, he had to explain *where* the play was taking place and *what* was happening.

These are some of the facts he gives us in the first four lines:

- It's about two 'households' (families)
- Both are 'alike in dignity' (important and powerful)
- They live in Verona (a town in northern Italy)
- They have an 'ancient grudge' (old feud or quarrel)
- This breaks into 'new mutiny' (more violence)
- 'civil blood makes civil hands unclean' (citizens kill each other).

Read the rest of the speech. What else is he saying? Which of the statements below are correct?

The families each have a child.

It's about lovers who kill themselves.

The lovers are cross-eyed.

There's a traffic jam on stage.

The lovers bury their parents.

Their deaths end their parents' quarrel.

This story will take us about two hours to tell.

Please listen carefully.

FEUDING FAMILIES

FRIENDS AND ENEMIES

The two rival families in *Romeo and Juliet* are the Montagues and the Capulets.

This diagram shows the families.

- ◎ With a partner, talk about where the other characters belong in or around the diagram.
- ◎ Sketch your own complete diagram to show characters' loyalties.
- ◎ Some might be harder to place than others!

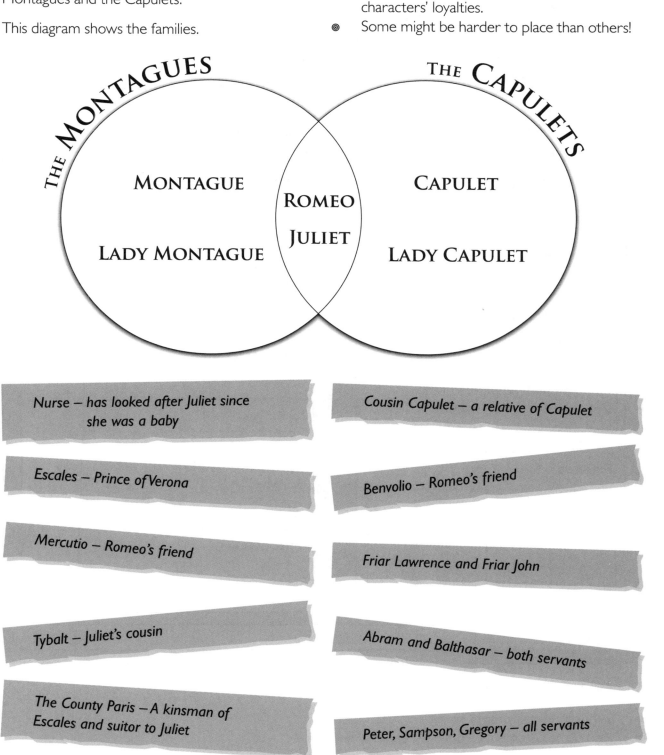

THE MONTAGUES

THE CAPULETS

MONTAGUE

LADY MONTAGUE

ROMEO
JULIET

CAPULET

LADY CAPULET

Nurse – has looked after Juliet since she was a baby

Cousin Capulet – a relative of Capulet

Escales – Prince of Verona

Benvolio – Romeo's friend

Mercutio – Romeo's friend

Friar Lawrence and Friar John

Tybalt – Juliet's cousin

Abram and Balthasar – both servants

The County Paris – A kinsman of Escales and suitor to Juliet

Peter, Sampson, Gregory – all servants

STAR-CROSSED LOVERS

MyScene *on the Net*

Romeo Montague – Yo!

My profile

Gender Male   **Age** 17

Profile views   **Share the luv**
100,000   ♥ 800

Hometown
Verona

Happiest when...
Hanging out with   Climbing
my mates   Acting
Gatecrashing parties   Writing poetry

I hate...   People who don't
The 'Caps'   stand up for their
Old fogeys   friends

The other half of me

I wish!

Rosaline
♥♥♥

My blog

Doing all the usual – keeping the folks happy at home, loads of fencing to keep fit, trying my best not to think of HER... My mates tell me there are plenty of other fish in the sea, but I'm not interested. There's a big bash tonight at the Caps. Might gatecrash just for a laugh, but don't really feel like it...

<u>Click here to read more</u>

Friends

Mercutio

Benvolio

Comments

<u>Bands</u>   <u>Video box</u>   <u>Photos</u>

This could be Romeo's page on a social networking site.

◎   When in the play might he have written this?
◎   Add some comments from Mercutio and Benvolio.
◎   How would Romeo update it later in the play?

In the Chorus, the lovers are described as 'star-crossed'. It means that their fate is doomed because the stars – which Elizabethans believed predicted lives – are at odds. It's a bit like horoscopes today, which tell us what's likely to happen according to our star sign.

◎ Do you think there's any truth in star signs?

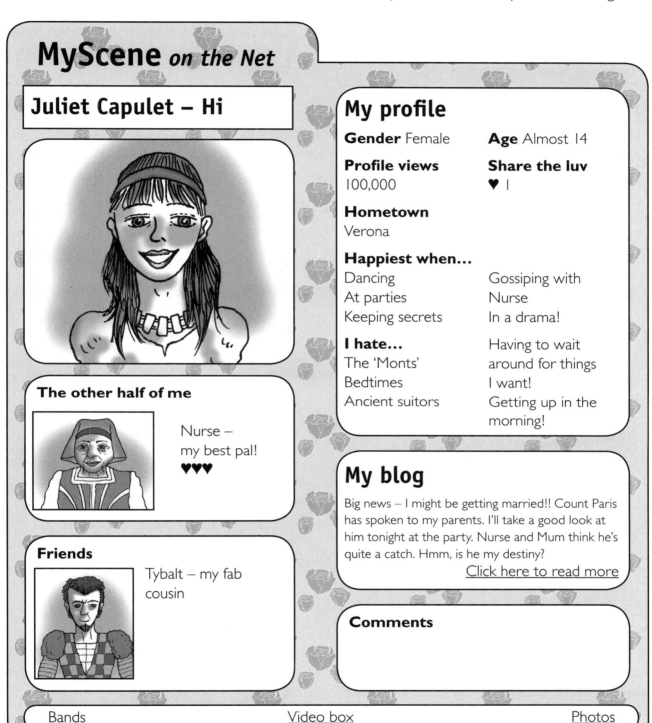

MyScene *on the Net*

Juliet Capulet – Hi

The other half of me

Nurse – my best pal!
♥♥♥

Friends

Tybalt – my fab cousin

My profile

Gender Female   **Age** Almost 14

Profile views   **Share the luv**
100,000   ♥ 1

Hometown
Verona

Happiest when...
Dancing   Gossiping with
At parties   Nurse
Keeping secrets   In a drama!

I hate...   Having to wait
The 'Monts'   around for things
Bedtimes   I want!
Ancient suitors   Getting up in the
                           morning!

My blog

Big news – I might be getting married!! Count Paris has spoken to my parents. I'll take a good look at him tonight at the party. Nurse and Mum think he's quite a catch. Hmm, is he my destiny?

<u>Click here to read more</u>

Comments

<u>Bands</u>   <u>Video box</u>   <u>Photos</u>

This could be Juliet's page on a social networking site.

◎ When in the play might she have written this?

◎ Add a comment from Tybalt.

◎ How might Juliet update it later in the play?

◎ Write a MyScene page for another character, near the end of the play.

FOUR-DAY DRAMA

WHAT HAPPENS WHEN?

Shakespeare squeezes the action of the play into just four days: it starts early on Sunday morning, and ends early on Thursday morning.

- ◉ Look carefully at the sequence of events below.
- ◉ Decide where the ones at the bottom fit in the grid.

Sunday	Monday	Tuesday	Wednesday/Thursday
Street brawl	Friar agrees to marry the lovers.	Juliet is told she is to marry Paris.	Juliet appears to be dead.
Capulets plan a feast.	The nurse brings the message to Juliet.		Juliet is taken to family vault.
	Romeo and Juliet marry.		

Mercutio and Tybalt are killed.

Romeo and Juliet die.

Romeo and friends plan a masquerade.

Romeo is banished.

Romeo kills Paris at the vault.

Balcony scene: Romeo and Juliet declare their love.

Romeo and Juliet spend one night together.

Friar Lawrence gives Juliet a sleeping potion.

Hearing of Juliet's death, Romeo buys poison.

The Capulets and Montagues are united in their grief.

GATECRASHERS OR GUESTS?

Romeo and his friends plan a 'masquerade', i.e. visit the party in disguise, uninvited. This was quite common in the sixteenth century and hosts were often flattered that others wanted to come to their parties.

- ◉ What would be the pros and cons of a masquerade?
- ◉ Discuss with a partner whether you would ever gatecrash a party. Give reasons for your views.

FOUR-DAY DRAMA

READ ALL ABOUT IT!

BANISHED!
Former 'golden boy' Romeo Montague...

THE VAULT OF DEATH
Double suicide of young lovers...

FAMILY FEUD FLARES
Fighting broke out early Monday morning...

Newspaper headlines need to be short, punchy and attention-grabbing.

◎ Make up some more to report an event in the play.
◎ Write a short report, below a headline, about an event in the play. Include quotes from onlookers, and details of *who, when, where, what* and *why.*

THE BLAME GAME

Who was to blame for the tragedy of Romeo and Juliet?
Here are some viewpoints:

Tybalt is to blame. He picked a fight with Romeo, which led to him being banished.

Nurse should never have acted as messenger between Juliet and Romeo. Without her, the marriage wouldn't have taken place.

Friar Lawrence shouldn't have given Juliet the sleeping potion. That confused everyone.

Juliet's parents are to blame. The arranged marriage made Juliet desperate.

Play the blame game.
◎ In a group, each choose a character from the play.
◎ In turns, give reasons why you are NOT to blame for the tragedy.
◎ Vote for the person you feel is most to blame.

THE GENERATION GAP

"THE KIDS IN THE STORY ARE LIKE TEENAGERS TODAY." FRANCO ZEFFIRELLI

In 1968 Franco Zeffirelli made a film of *Romeo and Juliet*. He believed that Romeo and Juliet were like any other teenagers, at any time. Would you agree?

With a partner, do this quiz to help you decide.

		Teenagers today	Romeo and Juliet
1	Like to be with their friends	☐	☐
2	Fall in love	☐	☐
3	Can be fickle in relationships	☐	☐
4	Keep in touch easily by mobile and internet	☐	☐
5	May deceive their parents	☐	☐
6	Sometimes get into fights	☐	☐
7	Stand up for their friends	☐	☐
8	Like to keep some things private from their parents	☐	☐
9	Want different things to their parents	☐	☐
10	Can be very emotional	☐	☐
11	Can marry at 16, only with their parents' agreement	☐	☐

(Tick or cross each box, as you think appropriate.)

WHO STARTED IT?

Zeffirelli wanted to show how children pay for the errors that their parents make. Shakespeare describes the old quarrel as an 'ancient grudge'. Zeffirelli explains:

'The story is of two urchins crushed by a stupid, banal quarrel with origins even the adults don't know. In love the young couple found an ideal – one they could die for – and youth today is hungry for ideals.'

◉ Do you agree that young people are 'hungry for ideals' today? With a partner, jot down some arguments for and against.

Franco Zeffirelli directing the 1968 film version of Romeo and Juliet.

10

THE GENERATION GAP

TOO MUCH, TOO YOUNG!

In Act 1 Scene 2, Capulet and Paris discuss the possibility of Juliet's marriage.

◎ Read the extracts below.
◎ Match each one to its meaning in modern English.

Quotation

My child is yet a stranger in the world.

Younger than she are happy mothers made.

Let two more summers wither in their pride,
Ere we may think her ripe to be a bride.

And too soon marr'd are those so early made.

Modern English

And they are soon damaged by being such young mothers.

Let's wait two more years before we consider her ready to marry.

Some girls, younger than her, are happy to have children.

My child is still young and doesn't know much about life.

YOU WILL/I WON'T

'you baggage! You tallow-face!'

'you shall not house with me'

'speak not, reply not, do not answer me!'

'I'll not be forsworn'

'disobedient wretch'

'I will drag thee on a hurdle thither'

A family row blazes when Juliet refuses to marry Paris (Act 3 Scene 5). Lord Capulet is outraged.

◎ In small groups, imagine you are on a TV show which tries to resolve family arguments. One person should host the show, another takes on the role of Juliet and another the role of Lord Capulet. The rest of the group make up the audience who can ask questions or make suggestions.

'we have a curse in having her'

'what is mine shall never do thee good'

MIND YOUR LANGUAGE!

WATCH OR LISTEN?

Do you like to watch or listen to
your entertainment?

In Shakespeare's day there were no movies,
computers, photographs or TVs, so there
was far less to watch. People relied more on
entertainment through words and plays. This
meant that Shakespeare was big business!

QUOTING SHAKESPEARE

How many of these words and phrases do you
know and use?

I haven't slept a wink!

foul play

in a pickle

horrid

flesh and blood

good riddance

vanish into thin air

leapfrog

lonely

be cruel to be kind

zany

excellent

a tower of strength

send him packing

haven't slept a wink

They were all coined (made up) or made popular
by Shakespeare. So whenever they are said –
someone is quoting Shakespeare!

Fact box
- ◉ Shakespeare gave us over 2000
  new words.
- ◉ A tenth of the most popular quotations
  in English are from Shakespeare.

HAVING FUN

Shakespeare played with language to make his
audience laugh. He was the king of puns (jokes
using words with more than one meaning).

When Mercutio is slain, he jokes 'Ask for me
tomorrow and you will find me a grave man.'
- ◉ What are the two meanings of the
  word 'grave'?

Shakespeare played with words that sound similar.
In the opening few lines of the play we hear: *coals,
colliers, choler* and *collar.*
- ◉ Which sounds are repeated in each word?
- ◉ What does each word mean?

MIND YOUR LANGUAGE!

OXYMORONS – YOU MORON!

Shakespeare loved opposites and contrasts. He put unlikely ideas together. For example, as he leaves Juliet, Romeo says: 'parting is such sweet sorrow'. What do you think he means by this?

a) her hair parting is a big mistake
b) he is offering her a sweet as they part
c) it's hard to leave her, although he loves being in love

An **oxymoron** is the putting together of words that seem to contradict each other. Here are more from *Romeo and Juliet*:

'loving hate'

'heavy lightness'

'cold fire'

'sick health'

Make up some more oxymorons of your own using these words:

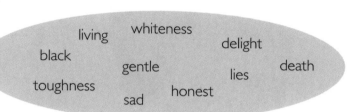

living   whiteness   delight
black   gentle   lies   death
toughness   honest
sad

IMAGINE...

Shakespeare used words to build up images (pictures) in the audience's mind. These images gave detail, personality and fun to ordinary descriptions. Match up the images to what is being said:

Shakespeare's images	What is being said
The grey-ey'd morn smiles on the frowning night	She stands out.
It seems she hangs upon the cheek of night As a rich jewel in an Ethiop's ear (description of Juliet)	I'm hidden by the darkness.
An hour before the worshipp'd sun Peer'd forth the golden window of the east	It is dawn.
I have night's cloak to hide me from their eyes	People have seen him there, crying and sighing.
Many a morning hath he there been seen, With tears augmenting the fresh morning's dew, Adding to clouds more clouds with his deep sighs	An hour before daybreak.

BEWARE!

Sometimes people think they know Shakespeare, but they get it wrong!

One of the most famous lines from the play is: 'O Romeo, Romeo, wherefore art thou Romeo?'

'Wherefore' doesn't mean *where*. It means *why!* Juliet is wishing Romeo wasn't called Romeo Montague, because this makes him her family's enemy.

Seen It?

Famous Romeos

In the 19th century some actors disliked playing Romeo as they thought the character was too effeminate. In some productions, women took the role of Romeo, to emphasize his youth (like the pantomime tradition of a woman taking on the 'hero' role).

More recently, Romeo has become a popular role and many actors have excelled in it. Do you recognize these Romeos?

People have different ideas about what Romeo should look like and the sort of character he should be.

◎ If you were a director, what sort of Romeo would you look for? List some key features, including looks and characteristics.

Answers

1 = David Tennant, 2 = Sean Bean,
3 = Ray Fearon, 4 = Leonardo Di Caprio

Seen It?

Famous films

The first *Romeo and Juliet* movie was made in 1900 by the French film maker Clement Maurice. It was in black and white and silent! Since then, film makers around the world have re-told the same story in their own way, changing the setting and interpreting the play in very different ways.

Here are three of the most famous films. Try to watch at least one of them, or extracts from two.

Fact File

Title: Romeo and Juliet

Director: Baz Luhrmann

Stars: Leonardo DiCaprio and Claire Danes

Date: 1996

Setting: (fictional) Verona Beach in California. The Capulets and Montagues have rival business empires. The action-packed, fast-paced movie includes gun shoot outs, car chases, drugs, police squads in helicopters and a tattooed priest.

Success: Box-office hit, winning many awards.

Fact File

Title: Romeo and Juliet

Director: Franco Zeffirelli

Stars: Leonard Whiting and Olivia Hussey

Date: 1968

Setting: Renaissance Italy
Real teenagers were cast in the leading roles, which caused some controversy but also made it popular with young audiences.

Success: Box-office hit, winning 4 Academy Awards

Fact File

Title: West Side Story (a musical)

Director: Jerome Robbins and Robert Wise

Music and songs: Leonard Bernstein and Stephen Sondheim

Date: 1961

Setting: 1950s New York slums, with rival gangs: the Jets (Americans) and Sharks (Puerto Ricans)

Success: Box-office hit, winning 10 Academy Awards

Where and when?

If you were making a film, retelling the story of *Romeo and Juliet*, what setting would you choose?

◎ Would you set it in the past, present or future?
◎ In which country or community would it be set?
◎ Who would be the rival gangs/families?
◎ At what sort of party would your hero and heroine meet?

15

POINTS OF VIEW

Although Shakespeare wrote *Romeo and Juliet* in the late 16th century, many of its themes and issues are still relevant today.

Here are a few of them, with some points of view:

DO YOU BELIEVE IN LOVE AT FIRST SIGHT?

Yes. Some people feel instant strong attraction for each other.

No. That's just physical infatuation, not love. It doesn't last.

WOULD YOU AGREE TO AN ARRANGED MARRIAGE?

Yes. I trust my parents to choose a suitable partner for me.

No. My parents can't possibly know who will make a good partner for me.

HOW FAR WOULD YOU GO TO STICK UP FOR YOUR FRIENDS?

All the way. If you don't fight for your mates, they won't fight for you.

I'd support them if I agree with them, but physical violence is a last resort.

With a partner, choose one of these issues and create a short role-play.
- ◎ Decide on a setting where the issue might arise.
- ◎ Choose two characters, to voice opposite viewpoints.
- ◎ List arguments that can be used on both sides.
- ◎ Rehearse, then perform your role-play.
- ◎ Ask your audience which character they agree with.